Michael Learns How To Make Money

Copyright 2015
Moor Gold Publishing

moo'r
PUBLISHING

ISBN-13: 978-0692460689
ISBN-10: 0692460683

Printed in The United States of America, 2015

Michael Learns How To Make Money

Written by
Zipporah Carter

Illustrated by
Award-Winning Artist
Rosemarie Gillen

moo'r
PUBLISHING

To Christian—my son, my genius, my anjewel.

One sunny afternoon, Michael had a wonderful birthday party. Everyone was having a great time. However, Michael still wasn't completely happy.

After the party, Michael pouted and whined to his Mom,
"I didn't get the GX video game that I wanted."

"Well, I'm sorry you didn't get enough for your birthday," mom replied. "But I'm going to teach you how to be a little more grateful, young man."

Then Mom said, "I'm going to teach you how to earn money to buy the things you want. When you earn them, you will become more grateful for things Mommy and Daddy do for you."

Mom grabbed her wallet and sat at the table with Michael and Dad. They pulled out some cash and showed him the different dollar bills and coins. They explained to him the different values of each.

"I'm going to start you off with a weekly allowance," said Mom. "You will have to keep your room clean if you want to continue to get your allowance every week."

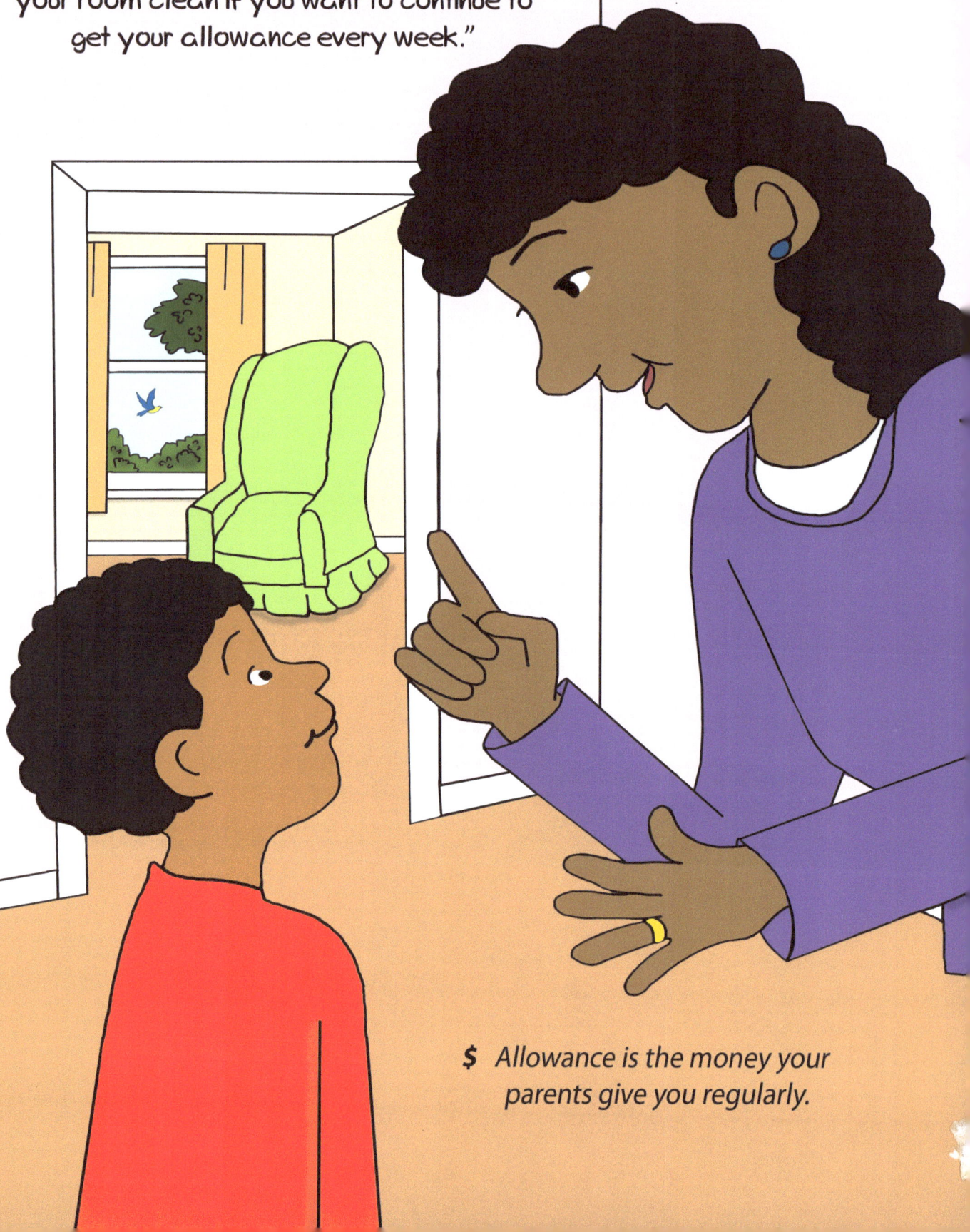

$ *Allowance is the money your parents give you regularly.*

"Here is $10 for the week," Mom said as she handed him the money. "Spend it wisely so you can save some of it afterwards to go towards your video game."

"Yes, Mom," he replied happily. He was so happy to have $10 to spend.

During the school day, Michael used his allowance money to buy snacks from the cafeteria.

$2.00

Michael continued to buy snacks at school throughout the week, and by the end of the week, he was left with only $3.

"How are you doing with your money, son?" his Mom asked.

"Well, I only have $3 left," said Michael. Sadly, he added, "I'll never save enough to buy the video game. It costs $100."

$ *How much money did Michael spend during the week if he only has $3.00 left?*

Hint: He started with $10.00

"Well, now it's time I teach you about investing your money,"
Mom said.

"Investing? What does that mean?" Michael asked curiously.

"Investing means spending your money to make more money,"
his Mom replied.

Mom added, "In other words, you buy something that will pay you more money back. This way you can earn more money. For example, you can buy lemons to sell lemonade, or buy toys to sell them for more money, and much more. These are just a few of the ways you can invest."

$ *Sell (or sold) means to give something away to someone so they can give you money back in return.*

"Wow. How cool! So, if I keep investing, I will be rich!"

"Possibly," Mom giggled. "But, slow down, son. Let's take it one step at a time."

Michael was so excited about the idea of making money that he began to think of ways he can invest.

"Aha! I can buy some new crayons and sell some of my awesome drawings. I can draw really well," he said to himself.

The Artist Shoppe

Michael went to the store and bought crayons and paper, which cost $3. This was his investment.

Michael was a little sad
that he didn't have any
money left. So to cheer
himself up, he started
drawing using the
crayons and paper
he'd just bought.

Game of Chance

It was a new week, and Michael earned his $10 allowance for keeping his room clean. He went to school with his money in his pocket and all of his drawings in his backpack ready to sell them. When he arrived at school, he showed all of his friends and his teacher his drawings.

He sold 8 drawings for $1 each that first week, which means he made a total of $8.

$ If Michael made $8 from selling his drawings, and only spent $3 investing in crayons and paper, how much EXTRA money did he gain just from investing his money?

Hint: $8 (he made from selling drawings)
     - $3 (he spent on crayons and paper)
     _____
     (extra money he made by investing)

Michael showed his Mom and Dad all of the money he made throughout the week.

"We are so proud of you!" they said, as they hugged him.

$ *How much did Michael have all together at the end of this week if he had $5 left over from spending his allowance money, and the $8 from selling his drawings?*

Hint: $5 *(left over from allowance)*
$+ $8 *(he made from selling drawings)*
_____
(total money at end of the week)

Michael continued to get his allowance and sell his drawings for a month. He made lots of money, so he decided to buy his parents a gift.

Penelope's Gift Shop

Summer Festival
Daisy Park
Come one, Come All

Food and Fun- June 6

"Thanks for teaching me about money," said Michael. He happily handed his parents the gift.

"Here! I bought this gift with the money I made to say thank you for everything you guys do for me. Now I understand how hard you work for your money and I'm thankful for everything."

"Thank you Michael!"
said Mom and Dad.

They were so happy to see the
gift Michael bought for them.

Then Dad said, "And son, we bought you a surprise also." Dad pulled out the GX video game. "We thought you deserved it. We're proud at how you've managed your money. You learned a very valuable lesson, son. Always keep these lessons in mind."

Michael continues to save and invest his money, and always has enough money for all the extra things he wants.

THE END

TIPS FOR PARENTS:

It is wise to start an allowance system with your child once they are old enough to count, add, and subtract. Fake money can be used as well to teach them basic financial principles.

Allow your child to make small purchases, and if using fake money, allow them to "buy" goodies around the house.

Practice transactions and giving back change.

Open up a savings account for your child and put small amounts in there monthly. A CD is even recommended.

Ensure that your child knows the values of dollars and coins.

Educate your child on ways to invest.

www.ingramcontent.com/pod-product-compliance
Lightning Source LLC
LaVergne TN
LVHW072102070426
835508LV00002B/225